# The Boy Who Was BOLD

**ADAM GRIFFIN**

Illustrations by Evelt Yanait

B&H kids
Brentwood TN

*For Oscar, Gus, and Theodore*
*as well as all their friends*
*at Eastside Community Church.*
*Shine like stars, kids!*

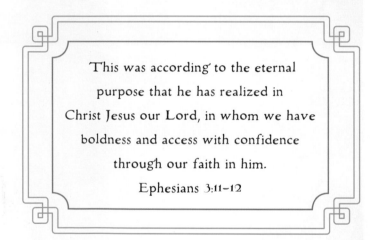

This was according to the eternal
purpose that he has realized in
Christ Jesus our Lord, in whom we have
boldness and access with confidence
through our faith in him.

Ephesians 3:11–12

Text copyright © 2023 by Adam Griffin.
Illustrations copyright © 2023 by B&H Publishing Group.
Published by B&H Publishing Group, Brentwood, Tennessee. All rights reserved.
978-1-0877-8843-2
Dewey Decimal Classification: C232.903
Subject Heading: JESUS CHRIST \ COURAGE \ BOLDNESS
Unless otherwise noted, Scripture quotations are taken from The Holy Bible, English Standard Version®.
Copyright © 2001 by Crossway Bibles, a publishing ministry of Good News Publishers.
Scriptures marked NIV are taken from the Holy Bible, New International Version®,
NIV® Copyright ©1973, 1978, 1984, 2011 by Biblica, Inc. Used by permission.
All rights reserved worldwide.
Printed in Dongguan, Guangdong, China, March 2023
1 2 3 4 5 6 7 • 27 26 25 24 23

In the temple one day, a boy not yet thirteen
had just gathered a crowd. He was causing a scene!
He was young but knew all of the Bible they read.
They were shocked by the questions and answers he said.

ESTHER

SAMSON

RUTH

He was fearless—like heroes
in tales God had told,
those true stories well-known
by the boy who was bold.

4

SHADRACH MESHACH ABEDNEGO

RAHAB

DANIEL

MOSES

DAVID

Those who came near to hear thought him odd. They were awed by how bravely this daring boy spoke about God.

"He's so young, sure, and wise," they all marveled with joy.
"By himself? Unafraid? That's one bold little boy!"

His dear mom named him Jesus, our God with us here.

Fully God, fully boy — he's God's Son coming near.

He grew into a man and grew even more bold.
What he said, whom he loved, all the things he foretold,
and the audacious mission he came to complete—
there has never been greater nor bolder a feat.

Jesus cherished the people whom nobody loved—
the rejected and hated, the pushed and the shoved.
Those with power observed him, and they were confused.

"Why would someone, a leader, pursue the abused?"

He spent time with and ate with and hugged the untouched.
Jesus welcomed the lonely and boldly did much
to remind every person that they had great worth
that exceeded the value of all life on earth.

His disciples were mocked, for they loved the ignored.
When the rest turned away, these few boldly turned toward.

There's a pressure that comes from the popular crowd
to be picky about where a friendship's allowed,
to avoid all the people who don't seem that great.
But for Jesus, his people, they stood against hate.

At times, Jesus taught God's Word to very large crowds.

Lots of them did not like it, but he remained loud.

He was never afraid of what had to be said.

He offended, so he was rejected widespread.

His concern was not pleasing a world that was wrong.

He was doing God's will, and that takes standing strong.

Jesus loved them so much that he would not conform.

He would urge and implore them, "Repent! Be transformed."

It is not that he aimed to be hated or shunned.
Being bold for our God just leaves some people stunned.
Jesus told them what he knew they needed to hear,
even when it made Jesus stand out and seem weird.

"Sin has sickened the world.
You can't make yourselves well.
The creation is groaning
and crying to tell
every heart, it is ill,
and there aren't any cures—
unless you will trust me.
I'll give my life for yours."

There is nothing so bold that you ever will find
than to face sin and death on behalf of mankind.

Yes, because of his love, his devotion to you,
he faced torture unspeakable, abandonment too,
so that we might have life because his heart was stopped.

We can hold our heads high because his crowned head dropped.

He was carried and buried by very few friends.
It seemed sure to those watching
that this was the end.

He was gone.

He had died.

He did just what he'd said.

Know what's truly fantastic?
He didn't stay dead!

He fought sin and fought death, and when three days were done,
he got up from the grave, for he'd faced them and won!
And now guess what's so great about seeing him win.
That Jesus invites YOU to be bold just like him!

We expect to be different, expect to be odd.

We expect to be strange now because we love God.

See, God's children are different, and we must know how
to stand up—be resilient when it's wrong to bow.
The world's dark; it needs light, and the turn now is ours.
In your time—yes, right now—in the dark, shine like stars!

As for you, here's your chance! Think of what you will do.
When it's time to be odd, will you stand? Be bold too?

Our God's people are fearlessly loyal to him.

We would rather do what God has asked than fit in.

When the crowd says to you, "Join our sin! It will please us!"

Let's refuse. Be steadfast, for we just follow Jesus.

Though the crowd is not with us, we know our God is!

We'll not flinch, not since now we know which way is his!

Let's be faithful and daring and brave. Never fold.
For it's our turn to be like the boy who was bold!

Since we have such a hope,
we are very bold.
2 Corinthians 3:12

## Remember

"Since we have such a hope, we are very bold." — 2 Corinthians 3:12

## Read

Read John 15:18–21 and John 16:33. Christians have a great mission, or calling, to tell the world the good news: God forgives sin. If you follow Jesus, you might stick out and be disliked by some people. Remember, Jesus experienced this too. It's okay if others think you are peculiar because you love God. God can make you so confident in his mission that even if other people dislike you, you'll go on fearlessly loving Jesus and loving them. Be brave and bold, friends. Jesus reminds us, "In this world you will have trouble. But take heart! I have overcome the world" (John 16:33 NIV).

## Think

1. Why didn't some people like Jesus?

2. What would you call someone who does the right thing even when it's unpopular?

3. If someone said to you, "I don't like what your family believes," what might you say to them?

4. It was probably hard for Jesus's mother, Mary, to hear so many people say hateful things about her son and then watch them hurt him. How do you think she felt when Jesus rose from the dead? How do you feel about his resurrection?

5. Because Jesus defeated sin and death for his people, Christians have hope that no one can take away. How does trusting Jesus change people's lives?